SPECIAL FORCES

Badger Publishing Limited
Oldmedow Road,
Hardwick Industrial Estate,
King's Lynn PE30 4JJ
Telephone: 01438 791037
www.badgerlearning.co.uk

2 4 6 8 10 9 7 5 3

Special Forces ISBN 978-1-78147-543-0

Text © Jonny Zucker 2014
Complete work © Badger Publishing Limited 2014

Publisher: Susan Ross
Senior Editor: Danny Pearson
Designer: Fiona Grant

Photos: Cover image: REX
Page 4: British Library/Robana/REX
Page 5: Stephen Mulcahey/Alamy
Page 6: Troy GB images/Alamy
Page 9: Rossella Apostoli/Alamy
Page 10: Universal History Archive/Un/REX
Page 13: www.canadaatwar.ca
Page 15: Ray Warhurst/Daily Mail/REX
Page 16: Moviestore Collection/REX
Page 17: c.Col Pics/Everett/REX
Page 19: ITV/REX
Page 22: Andrew Chittock/Alamy
Page 24: Jack Sullivan/Alamy
Page 27: Image Broker/REX
Page 29: Moviestore Collection/REX
Page 31: Sipa USA/REX

Attempts to contact all copyright holders have been made.
If any omitted would care to contact Badger Learning, we will be happy to make appropriate arrangements.

Contents

1. Special forces in the ancient world

Ancient China

The idea of giving small groups of soldiers special training goes back a very long way. In the 11th century BC, a Chinese military strategist, called Jiang Ziya, wrote about such men. He said specially chosen soldiers should be trained to climb the highest mountains and to cover long distances very quickly. These soldiers helped King Wen and King Wu overthrow the Shang Dynasty.

Jiang Ziya was a military expert in ancient China.

The Romans

In around 500 AD, the Romans selected the strongest soldiers for extra speed and strength training. These men were then placed on very small, fast, camouflaged boats. When the boats landed on enemy territory, the specially trained soldiers sped onto land to carry out spying missions. They then reported back on the enemy's positions and the number of troops they had.

Norse warriors

These warriors were very strong and tough. The toughest of these warriors were known as berserkers (or berserks). They went into battle in what appeared to be an uncontrollable, trance-like fury. They were said to be almost unstoppable and would carry on fighting even if severely injured.

Some historians believe that berserkers worked themselves into a rage before battle. Others think that they might have eaten drugged foods or drunk a large amount of alcohol!

Ancient Japan

In 15th and 16th century Japan, groups of soldiers who had undergone special training were known as 'ninjas'. These men were incredibly fast and strong fighters. They were used to spy on enemy positions as well as to smash enemy equipment and supplies. Ninjas were also used as bodyguards for military leaders.

Ninjas did not traditionally wear the black shown in modern books and films. They usually dressed in everyday clothes so no one knew they were ninjas.

They would carry a hidden sword, known as a *katana*, as well as ropes and grappling hooks. They also carried a *Tenugui* – a piece of cloth that could cover their face (to protect their identity), form a belt or be used in climbing.

Ninjas often dressed in disguise to spy on people and carry out their attacks. They have been known to dress as priests, fortune tellers, monks and merchants.

2. Modern special forces

The first special forces

The British army started using special forces in the 1840s. In the Boer War of 1899-1902, Britain used adult teams of scouts, such as the Lovat Scouts from Scotland. These teams were skilled in:

- shooting
- military tactics
- 'field crafts' – things like setting up camps, hunting and surviving in the wild.

The First World War (1914-1918)

During the First World War, ANZAC (The Australian and New Zealand Army Corps) and Canada provided special forces to fight alongside regular British army troops. These soldiers specialised in lightning quick raids on enemy trenches and capturing enemy soldiers. They were known for their bravery, speed and strength.

The Second World War (1939-1945)

It was in the Second World War that special forces really came into their own. The British Prime Minister, Winston Churchill, asked military leaders to create: *"Specially trained troops of the hunter class who can develop a reign of terror down the enemy coast."* He wanted special soldiers who could operate on land, by sea and in the air.

These special soldiers were trained to survive in incredibly hot deserts and travel huge distances in very fast times. They were used in the Burma Campaign, where conditions were very tough.

The British army also formed 'Inter-Allied' special forces units that consisted of 'special' soldiers from Britain, France, Belgium, Norway, the Netherlands and Poland.

In 1941, America joined World War Two on the side of Britain and the Allies. The Americans trained soldiers to operate deep behind enemy lines without being discovered. America and Canada also set up the First Special Service Force – which was known as the 'Devil's Brigade'. These daring troops took part in high altitude ski sabotage missions in Norway.

British special forces were used to parachute behind enemy lines in Germany and occupied France. They took part in many missions, which included blowing up bridges to stop the German army's advance. They also attacked communication systems and freed prisoners. Many of their stories only came to light 30 or 40 years after the war had ended.

WOW! facts

The members of the Devil's Brigade had to be trained quickly to carry out their missions in Norway. They learned to parachute two days after they arrived at the training camp, and they learned to ski in two weeks.

3. James Bond

James Bond author, Ian Fleming, was an important member of British Special Forces during WW2. He was involved in both 30 Assault Unit and T-Force Unit. Both of these were special units whose main aims were to steal enemy documents, learn about enemy technology and feed the Nazis misinformation about Britain's strategy.

After the war, Fleming told friends he wanted to write a spy novel. In 1952, he created a new special forces spy character called James Bond. He based Bond on all of the daring and brave special forces troops he had come across in the Second World War. He made Bond a commander in the Royal Naval Reserve and gave him the code name 007. The first Bond book was called *Casino Royale*.

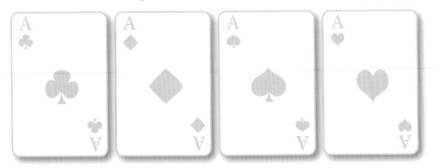

Ian Fleming wrote the James Bond novels.

The James Bond films contain hundreds of references to UK Special Forces. *Skyfall* even features a bomb blowing up the MI6 headquarters on the banks of the River Thames. After the Harry Potter films, the James Bond franchise is the most successful in the world. The James Bond films have made over £3.7 billion.

Daniel Craig, who played James
Bond in the most recent films, performs
many of his own stunts. These include a
fight scene on top of a moving train and
jumping out of a window onto a bus.

4. Special forces today

The SAS

After World War Two, Britain and America decided to build up their special forces units. Army leaders liked the idea of having small specialised units of men who could get in and out of enemy territory far quicker than a large brigade. The British SAS (Special Air Service) was formally created in 1950.

The SAS became world famous after the Iranian Embassy siege in 1980. Terrorists had taken over the Iranian Embassy in London with 26 hostages.

On the sixth day of the siege, people around the world watched on TV as SAS troops abseiled from the roof of the building and smashed through the windows.

In 17 minutes they saved all but one of the hostages and killed five of the six terrorists.

Joining the SAS

To become a member of today's SAS you have to get through an incredibly tough training process. This includes exercises in very hot and very cold weather, both in daylight and at night. Trainees need to be able to go for many hours without food or water and spend a lot of time learning to abseil, climb walls and break into heavily guarded buildings. Very few people make it through all of the tests.

Weapons and kit

In terms of kit, members of the SAS carry HK MP5 sub machine guns and Sig Sauer pistols. Some also carry a Remington shotgun loaded with 'Hatton' rounds. These are very good for shooting off door hinges without putting lives at risk.

Torches are often attached to these weapons so that soldiers have much clearer vision in night-time settings.

Other pieces of SAS equipment include:

- AC100 armoured helmet
- stun grenades
- gas mask
- abseil harness
  (for climbing down buildings)
- frame charges
  (for blowing up walls and doors)
- thermal lances
  (for cutting through cables)
- bulletproof armoured waistcoat
- plasticuffs
  (to tie prisoners' hands)
- glow sticks
  (to mark off safe areas)

For an assault on a building, plane or camp, the SAS use specially adapted Land Rovers and Range Rovers. These have secure communications systems. They are fitted with extended ladders attached to the roof racks. The soldiers cling to the sides of the cars on special hand-holds or are stacked up on the assault ladders. The vehicles approach their targets at incredibly fast speeds.

WOW! facts

Unlike in the regular army, SAS soldiers do not call each other by rank names like 'Sergeant'. This is so that if the troops are captured, the enemy won't know who the leader is and won't treat them more harshly than the others. Members of SAS units are often known by nicknames.

5. UK Special Forces

The SAS may be the most famous British special force but it is only one part of UKSF (UK Special Forces). UKSF also includes:

- The Special Boat Service
- The Special Reconnaissance Regiment
- The Special Forces Support Group
- The 18 (UKSF) Signal Regiment
- The Joint Special Forces Aviation Wing

All of these troops are under the command of the Director, Special Forces.

The **Special Reconnaissance Regiment** has the job of checking out locations before a special forces mission is carried out. Members of this force spy on people and places, and listen to covert recordings of enemies talking to or emailing each other. It is the only UK Special Forces unit that recruits women.

Like the SAS, the **Special Boat Service** can also trace its origins to World War Two. Today it has various squadrons or teams. Squadron S specialises in working with mini-submarines and small boats. M Squadron works in maritime counter-terrorism. This involves launching attacks on water-based terrorists and intercepting ships carrying suspect cargo, for example ingredients for bomb making or heavy weapons.

Behind the scenes

While Special Forces work 'on the ground', they receive massive back up from other military personnel.

In Britain, Special Forces are supported by two agencies: MI5 provides information and back up for issues and actions within the UK, while MI6 looks after missions in foreign countries.

In the United States, Special Forces are aided by the CIA (Central Intelligence Agency), the Department of Homeland Security and other agencies.

In times of national or international crisis in the UK, a special committee called Cobra meets.

This committee includes the Prime Minister as well as military leaders.

The role of British Special Forces is often discussed at these meetings and Cobra has the power to launch Special Forces missions if they feel they are necessary.

If trouble breaks out in one country, special forces from another country can travel very quickly to offer their help to the country under attack.

High-level members of different countries' special forces meet regularly to discuss tactics, state-of-the art weaponry and intelligence gathering methods.

Cobra is so named because the special meetings often take place in **C**abinet **O**ffice **B**riefing **R**oom **A**, in Whitehall, London.

6. Special forces books and films

Special forces appear in many fiction books. Ex-SAS paratrooper, Andy McNab, is the most famous writer on this theme. While he was in the SAS he was kidnapped, shot at and bombed. His first book, *Bravo Two Zero*, was an international bestseller.

During his time in the SAS, Andy McNab commanded a mission to destroy underground communication links in Iraq. He and some of the other men were captured and held for six weeks. When he was released, he was badly injured and ill but he was back on active service within six months.

Chris Ryan is another ex-special forces author. He served with Andy McNab in the SAS.

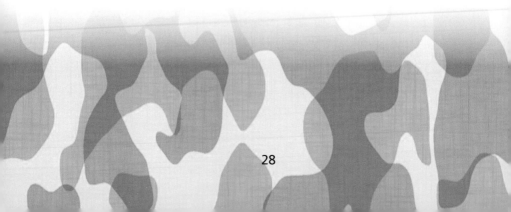

Many films have been made about special forces operations, including *Black Hawk Down*, *Navy SEALs* and *The Delta Force*.

Battle Los Angeles is about a US special forces unit battling an invasion of earth. *GI Jane* concerns the activities of a female soldier recruited into an all-male special forces unit.

Black Hawk Down, a film about American special forces carrying out operations in war-torn Africa, is based on a true story.

7. UK Special Forces Reserves

To be a part of UK Special Forces you don't have to be a full-time soldier. The UK Special Forces Reserves are volunteers who often have no previous military training.

To be accepted, you have to pass several physical and psychological tests and you have to be between 18 and 32 years old. To join the Reserves you must agree to spend a large portion of your time training and be willing to travel overseas at short notice.

In most jobs it would not be possible to commit to these terms, so normally Reserves do jobs where there is a lot of flexibility.

Special Forces also use volunteer support staff. They need people to work as drivers, chefs, vehicle mechanics and office workers. Medical staff are required, too, but people who want to volunteer must have had some military experience or be trained in emergency response or nursing.

Index